Balboa Press books may be ordered through booksellers or by contacting:

Balboa Press
A Division of Hay House
1663 Liberty Drive
Bloomington, IN 47403
www.balboapress.com
1 (877) 407-4847

ISBN: 978-1-9822-0709-0 (sc)
978-1-9822-0708-3 (e)

Print information available on the last page.

Balboa Press rev. date: 08/22/2018

BALBOA®
PRESS
A DIVISION OF HAY HOUSE

Starlight Seeds of Creation

Love Grows Love

Sri Lakshmi Oshun

There once was a Tiny Seed,

Within it contained all that it could be.

Inside it held infinite possibility.

Would it grow into a great big tree?

Perhaps a flower to befriend a honey bee,

Maybe a hot pepper or a little sweet pea.

All the seed knew, was it had all it would need,

And to grow into its full potential was its destiny.

From the dust of a comet the starlight seed came down,

To the Earth, and on the wind, it was carried around.

Until one day it landed and sank into the ground.

Cozy and warm, deep in the soil, Tiny Seed did dream and dwell.

Listening to the songs of the crystals, while Mother Earth held

Tiny Seed close to her Heart.

Singing to the seed, all the things it would need to start,

A journey that would take great courage and might.

A journey from darkness to find the light.

"One day, Tiny Seed you will grow into all that you can be,

just keep growing and you will see."

Tiny Seed smiled, as it felt Mother Earth's heart beat.

Dancing to the music of life, one day the Sun, Tiny Seed would greet!

Starting small, with baby steps, the Tiny Seed began to grow,

A little bit more each day, Tiny Seed began to learn and know.

About it's true nature and gifts to share,

To break through it's seed pod, Tiny Seed did prepare.

Tiny Seed gathered all it's energy, and transformed into a sprout!

Little Sprout burst through the soil, and began to peek out.

It pushed through the Earth, through a tiny little crack,

Little Sprout smiled to the Sun and the Sun smiled back!

Little Sprout's first moment meeting the Sun, was LOVE at first sight,

Joyfully singing "Ahhhuuumm," as it first saw the light.

Rejoicing in the beauty of life,

Little Sprout was so grateful to be alive!

Sending its roots down into the ground,

Little Sprout brought back all the life force it found.

Reaching for the sky, using it's strength to grow tall,

Little Sprout would try to be the best it could be, by giving it's all!

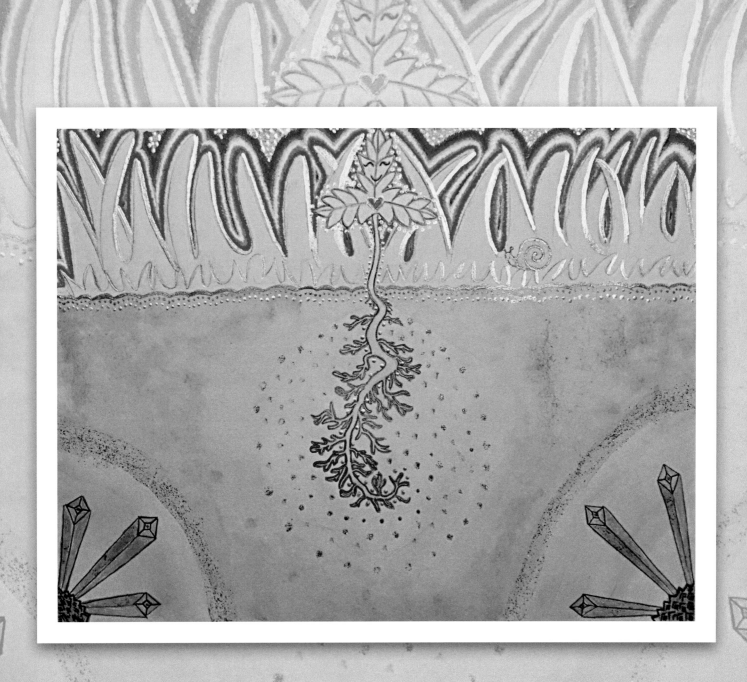

When seeing Little Sprout, the clouds rained down joyful tears,

Little Sprout drank the water, and released all its fears.

Feeling its connection to everything, Little Sprout gave thanks for life

Once a Tiny Seed in darkness; now a Little Sprout growing towards the light.

Remembering its true destiny, Little Sprout realized it was a Tree!

It grew bark, and branches, a strong trunk and many leaves.

Little Sprout was now a Young Sapling, growing more each day.

Not quite a full grown tree, but well on it's way!

Young Sapling's roots grew deep and strong,

As it grew it remembered Mother Earth's song.

She sang through the wind rustling leaves,

The rhythm of the rain, and the bubbling springs.

Young Sapling was grateful for the wisdom shared.

Feeling how much Mother Earth cared,

For each any every being carrying love in their heart.

When Mother Earth shared her stories, Young
Sapling would remember every part.

She would tell stories of the water, wind, fire and sky

Of the many forests and animals that you can find..

Butterflies, Bunnies, Dolphins and Deer,

Eagles, Elephants, Frogs and even Faeries appear.

Hummingbirds, Hippos, Tigers and Turtles,

Giraffes, Goldfish, Spiders and Squirrels!

From the high deserts to the deep oceans, Mother Earth loves all equally

And she loves to see all her children living in harmony.

Young Sapling would listen, soaking in all the love,

Filling up from the Earth below and Sun above.

Gentle Breeze would kiss Young Sapling goodnight,

As nightingales sang songs till their hearts delight.

The stars twinkled, winking from a diamond sky,

As rainbow star beings would dance and fly by.

At dawn many birds would gather in Young Saplings branches, singing to the rising Sun.

The warmth of the first light awakens all, as the day has just begun.

On this day, Young Sapling gave thanks and praise from the mountains to the sea,

For on this day, Young Sapling graduated to become a Mighty Oak Tree!

Mighty Oak watched the seasons come and go,

Winter, spring, summer and fall, through it all Mighty Oak had come to know,

What it means to give thanks and give back,

Living in abundance, never in lack.

For the grace of love touches all,

The four leggeds, two leggeds, flyers, swimmers, and those that crawl.

Those who live in harmony and come humbly to receive,

The blessing, of a Tiny Seed.

With many brothers and sisters in the branches; in the sunshine they would soak.

Little Acorn was born as a gift from Mighty Oak.

Imprinted with its destiny, containing all it would need,

Each one carrying on the legacy, of a Mighty Oak Tree.

Each a miracle of life, all within a Tiny Seed.

Journey from the darkness to find the light,

Along the way learn wrong from right.

Keep growing with all your might,

Never give up, be all you can be,

You are a unique and precious Tiny Seed.

You will be surprised on how far you can reach,

For we all have the potential to be a Mighty Oak Tree!

What you give you shall receive,

Share your gifts and sew your seeds.

Live in Harmony,

Walk in Beauty,

Give thanks to the Earth and the Heavens above.

Keep a song in your heart, as Love Grows Love.

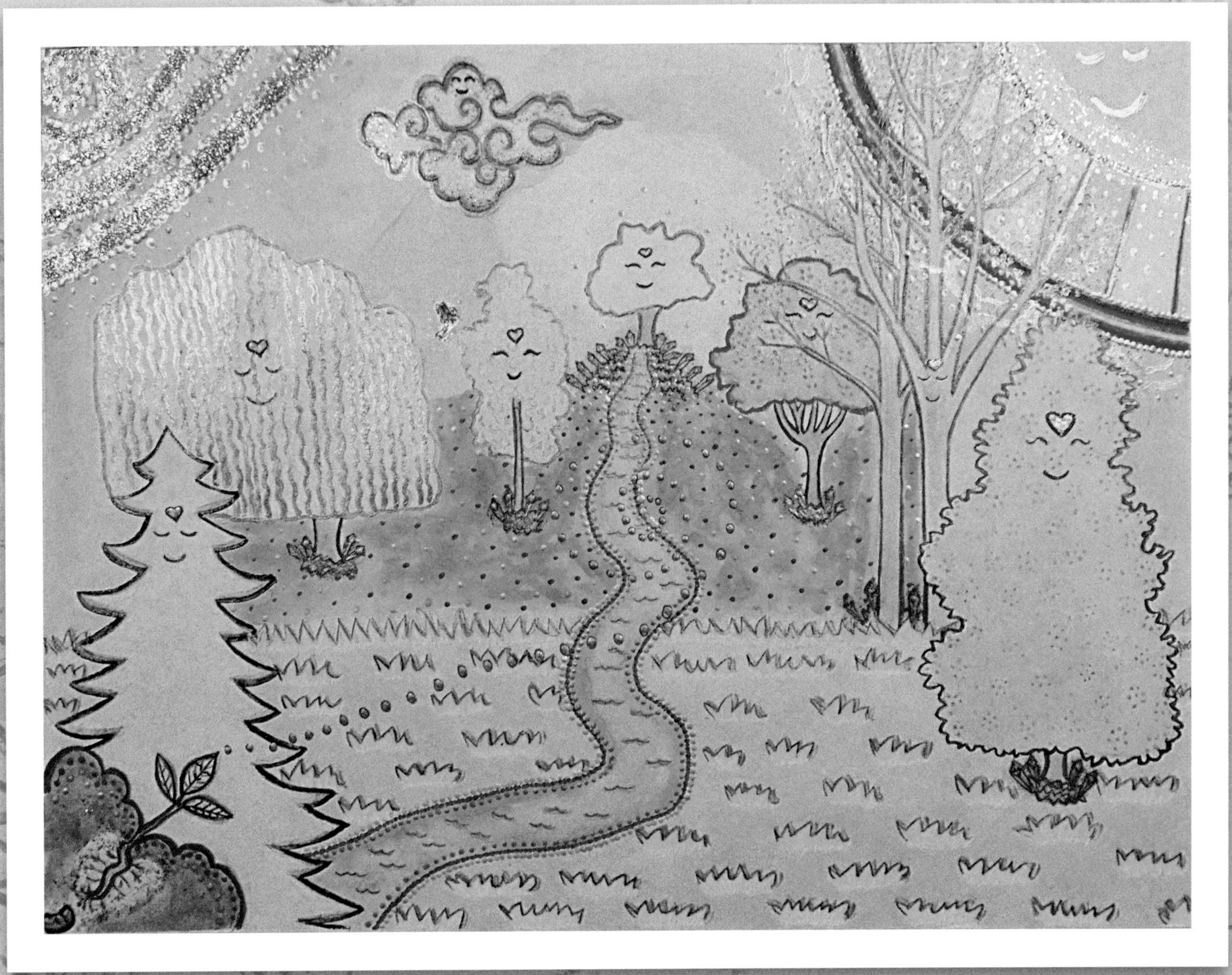

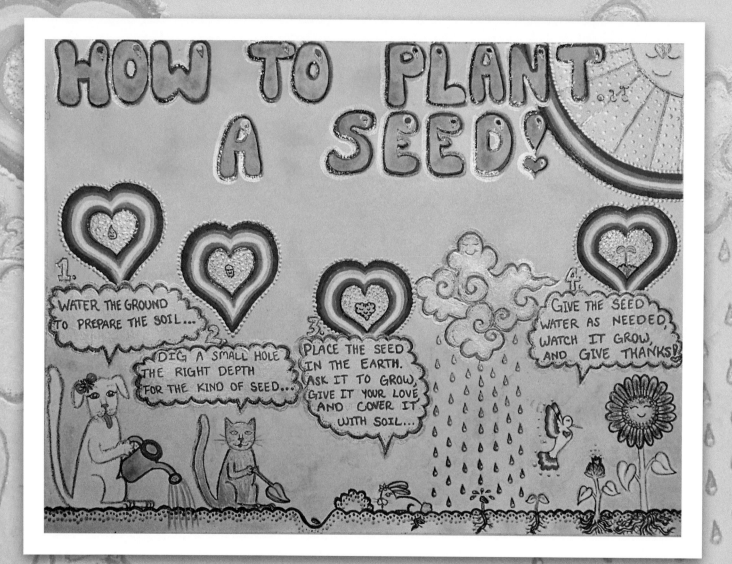

Lakshmi is a singer-songwriter, dancer and artist, originally from Santa Cruz, CA. She loves to garden and help things grow. She has worked with children for many years teaching dance, movement and music. She wrote "Starlight Seeds of Creation: Love Grows Love" to inspire children to connect with Mother Earth, and learn how to cultivate a life-long relationship with Nature, starting with the magic of one seed. Witnessing the journey of a seed from planting to harvest, is something Lakshmi would love all beings to get to experience. The joy from giving back to the Earth and learning how to live in harmony is the greatest reward. May all children know the truth, be free to grow into all they can be and be given the guidance to live in a good way aligned with LOVE.

Printed in the United States
By Bookmasters